A BUSINESS APPROACH TO LEMON FARMING

I0429942

Complete Entrepreneurial Step By Step Guide To Lemon Garden From Scratch

ZHURI HART

Copyright © [Zhuri Hart] [2024].

All rights reserved. This book, titled [Your Book Title], is protected by copyright law. No part of this publication may be reproduced, distributed, or transmitted in any form or by any means, including photocopying, recording, or other electronic or mechanical methods, without the prior written permission of the publisher, except in the case of brief quotations embodied in critical reviews and certain other noncommercial uses permitted by copyright law.

DISCLAIMER

This book is intended to provide general information and insights on adopting a business approach to farming. The content within is based on the author's knowledge and experiences up to the date of publication. It is essential to recognize that the field of agriculture is dynamic, influenced by various factors such as market conditions, climate, and regulatory changes.

Readers are advised to conduct thorough research, seek professional advice, and consider their unique circumstances before implementing any strategies or practices discussed in this book. The author and publisher disclaim any responsibility for the accuracy, completeness, or suitability of the information provided. The book is not a substitute for professional advice, and the author and publisher shall not be liable for any damages or losses arising from the use or reliance on the information presented herein.

Individual results may vary, and success in farming enterprises is contingent upon numerous variables. The author encourages readers to consult with relevant experts, agricultural extension services, and legal or financial professionals to tailor strategies to their specific needs and local conditions.

This book is not intended to be a comprehensive guide to all aspects of farming, and readers should exercise their judgment and discretion in applying the principles discussed. The author and publisher do not endorse any specific products, services, or companies mentioned in this book unless explicitly stated.

By reading this book, the reader acknowledges and accepts the inherent uncertainties in agricultural endeavors and agrees to use the information at their own risk.

TABLE OF CONTENTS

ABOUT THE BOOK

"A Business Approach to Lemon Farming," a book, offers a thorough manual for people who want to start and run a profitable lemon farming business. This book is significant because it successfully blends business knowledge with agricultural experience to present a comprehensive picture of Lemon growing as a successful enterprise. The book's main points are outlined in the paragraphs that follow.

The book concentrates on building a solid foundation by outlining the different lemon kinds, climate, and soil needs that are necessary for effective cultivation, as well as stressing the historical development of lemon farming. The book makes sure that readers are ready for the practical aspects of managing a lemon farm by offering insights into the instruments and equipment needed for lemon growing.

The book explores the commercial aspects of growing lemons, going beyond the technical aspects of gardening. Readers are assisted in creating a strategic plan for their lemon farming firm with chapters on financial planning, market research, and business planning. Setting reasonable objectives and benchmarks is emphasized to provide a workable and realistic road map for success.

Readers will receive comprehensive guidance on practical matters, including site selection, land preparation, and irrigation systems, enabling them to make well-informed decisions on their lemon orchards. The book also offers disease and insect management techniques, which are essential for maintaining the well-being and yield of lemon plants.

A thorough examination of planting and caring for lemon trees is provided, including information on fertilizer management, pruning strategies, planting protocols, and methods of propagation. Any farming operation must include harvesting and post-harvest handling.

This book provides in-depth information on when to harvest, how to harvest, how to handle crops after harvest, how to store crops, how to maintain quality, and how to grade.

The book's focus on marketing methods, which helps users identify target customers, build a brand for their lemon farm, and create successful marketing campaigns, is as significant. To make sure that the generated lemons efficiently reach the desired markets, various distribution networks, and sales tactics are investigated.

The book is devoted to discussing the difficulties faced by lemon growers, as well as risk management, contingency planning, and sustainable agricultural methods. Aspiring business owners in the sector can find inspiration and insightful lessons from the case studies and success stories of successful lemon producers.

Modern farming must take environmental concerns and regulatory compliance into account. This book delves into the nuances of agricultural regulations, environmental compliance, safety requirements, and best practices. The book also explores current technology, organic and sustainable farming practices, and advancements in lemon cultivars and types as well as future directions in lemon farming.

"A Business Approach to Lemon Farming" is an extensive manual that connects the administration of businesses with the growing of lemons. With its focus on both scientific and business factors, the book gives readers the information and abilities they need to start and run a profitable lemon farming business.

CHAPTER ONE

LEMON FARMING INTRODUCTION

AN OVERVIEW OF THE BUSINESS OF LEMON FARMING

Due to its economic importance and benefits to agriculture, lemon farming has become a successful and sustainable business. This review explores the various facets of lemon farming as a company, examining its complexities and the crucial role it plays in the agricultural industry as well as the larger economy.

Growing lemon trees to produce lemons is known as "lemon farming," and it has become increasingly popular among farmers and businesspeople. Citrus fruits are a mainstay of agribusiness activities due to their many uses in the culinary, medical, and industrial realms. A variety of tasks are involved in growing lemons, including choosing appropriate cultivars, planting, caring for the trees, gathering fruit, and selling the finished product.

LEMON FARMING'S SIGNIFICANCE FOR AGRICULTURE AND THE ECONOMY

The significance of lemon farming extends beyond the confines of specific farming operations, exerting a substantial influence on the wider agricultural terrain and the domestic economy.

Lemons are a high-value crop that is vital to agro-industrial growth and food security, in addition to improving farmers' financial standing. Lemon farming is made more economically viable by the fruit's versatility, which may be used for anything from fresh consumption to the creation of juices, essential oils, and by-products.

Lemon farming is unique in agriculture in that it can reduce the hazards associated with monoculture and diversify sources of revenue.

Lemon farmers profit from the hardiness of citrus trees, which are frequently more resilient and resistant to specific pests and diseases than other crops.

By lowering reliance on chemical inputs, this resilience not only guarantees farmers a more steady income but also encourages sustainable farming practices.

Moreover, the economic benefit of lemon farming includes the creation of jobs, especially in areas where citrus growing is the main agricultural industry. From farming to processing and distribution, the whole value chain generates employment possibilities, assisting rural livelihoods and promoting economic development.

Thus, lemon farming acts as a stimulus for socioeconomic development, particularly in places where there may not be many other employment options.

The summary of lemon farming as a company concludes by highlighting its importance in both the agricultural and commercial spheres. Growing lemons is more than just growing a popular citrus fruit; it's an integral part of a holistic agribusiness strategy that benefits both individual and community economic prosperity as well as the sustainability of agricultural methods. As we look deeper into the nuances of lemon farming, it becomes clear that its significance extends beyond the groves and orchards, influencing the agricultural and economic landscape on a larger scale.

CHAPTER TWO

KNOWING HOW TO CULTIVATE LEMONS

THE EVOLUTION AND HISTORY OF LEMON FARMING

Lemon cultivation has a long history that can be traced back to Southeast Asia centuries ago. It is thought that lemon cultivation originated in the Indus Valley and expanded throughout Persia and the Mediterranean region. Lemons were prized in ancient cultures not just for their culinary use but also for their medicinal and decorative properties. The expansion of commercial routes and exploration contributed to the globalization of lemon farming.

With improvements in breeding and cultivation methods, lemon farming had a substantial change over time. In Europe, the citrus industry—which includes lemons—grew throughout the Renaissance. Lemons were introduced to the Americas by Christopher Columbus and other explorers, and this was a major factor in the global integration of this citrus fruit into many cultures and cuisines.

CHARACTERISTICS OF DIFFERENT LEMON VARIETIES

Lemons are incredibly diverse; there are several types grown all over the world, and they all have unique qualities. Among the most popular are the Eureka and Lisbon types, which are prized for their vivid yellow hue, tangy taste, and adaptability in cooking. Meyer lemons, on the other hand, are valued for their thin, fragrant skin and have a sweeter flavor, which makes them a popular choice for cooking and dessert preparation.

Ponderosa, Villafranca, and Femminello are among the more notable kinds. The sizes, shapes, acidity levels, and climatic tolerance of these varietals vary.

 Farmers frequently select lemon cultivars according to the desired market, soil type, and climate of the area.

CONDITIONS OF THE SOIL AND CLIMATE FOR EFFECTIVE LEMON FARMING

Tropical and subtropical regions are ideal for growing lemons, and certain temperature ranges are necessary for this. In general, lemons thrive best in temperatures ranging from 21 to 38 degrees Celsius (70 to 100 degrees Fahrenheit).

Lemon trees are susceptible to frost, thus it's important to stay out of really cold locations. Lemon trees must receive enough sunlight; ideally, they should get at least 8 hours every day.

A soil that drains well and is neutral to slightly acidic is essential for growing lemons. It is best to choose loamy or sandy loam soil types since they ensure good drainage and avoid soggy situations that could damage the roots. Farmers can maintain the ideal pH level for growing lemons by conducting routine soil tests. Mulching the area around the tree bases helps keep weeds out and retain moisture.

ESSENTIAL EQUIPMENT AND TOOLS FOR GROWING LEMONS

To ensure effective agricultural methods, a collection of basic instruments and equipment is needed for lemon production. Deadwood removal, air circulation improvement, and tree shape maintenance all require pruning shears. Harvesting implements, such as hand harvesters or picking poles, make it easier to carefully take ripe fruit without endangering the trees.

Lemon trees benefit from irrigation methods, such as soaker hoses or drip irrigation, which help control the water flow and maintain a constant moisture level without flooding. Spreaders for fertilizer help distribute nutrients in the soil in an even manner. Farmers must wear protective clothing, such as hats and gloves, to protect themselves from the sun and thorns while performing jobs like harvesting and trimming.

CHAPTER THREE

ORGANIZING YOUR LEMON FARM ENTERPRISE

CREATING A LEMON FARMING BUSINESS PLAN

One of the most important steps in starting a profitable lemon farm is writing a thorough business strategy. This document functions as a road map, detailing the goals, tactics, and operational specifics required for the expansion of the company. Important elements of the plan should include the target market identification, a thorough analysis of competitors, the mission and vision of the lemon farm, and a detailed description of the products and services offered. The business plan should also cover hiring needs, workforce levels, and a financial performance forecast for the given time frame.

ANALYSIS AND RESEARCH ON THE MARKET

Undertaking comprehensive market research is essential to comprehend the workings of the lemon-growing sector. This entails researching the wants, tastes, and trends of consumers. It is possible to efficiently modify the lemon farm's products to match market expectations by identifying potential clients and knowing their wants. In addition, competitive and industry trend analysis facilitates strategic positioning and differentiation. The market study ought to delve into distribution routes, pricing tactics, and possible obstacles to guarantee the lemon farm is adequately equipped to maneuver through the competitive terrain.

FINANCIAL PLANNING AND BUDGETING

Financial planning and budgeting are essential to running a profitable lemon-growing operation. A thorough budget should take into consideration possible revenue changes, continuous operating costs, and initial beginning costs. This covers costs for purchasing land, installing irrigation systems, purchasing equipment, hiring workers, and marketing. Contingency reserves are a necessary component of financial planning to handle unforeseen obstacles.

In addition, keeping track of earnings and outlays, making educated decisions, and maintaining the lemon farm's long-term financial stability all depend on the implementation of an efficient accounting system.

CREATING REASONABLE OBJECTIVES AND BENCHMARKS

Establishing attainable goals is essential to a lemon farm's success. Objectives ought to be time-bound, relevant, measurable, achievable, and specific (SMART). Setting milestones aids in measuring progress and maintaining focus, whether the goal is increasing market reach, improving product quality, or reaching a specific manufacturing volume. To ensure that goals are in line with the natural growth cycles of the lemon trees, it is critical to acknowledge the seasonality of lemon farming and consider it when creating goals. Consistently evaluating and modifying objectives in light of market developments and performance metrics will enhance the flexibility and durability of the lemon farm industry.

CHAPTER FOUR

CHOOSING AND SETTING UP THE SITE

CHOOSING THE IDEAL SITE FOR LEMON FARMING

Selecting the right place to grow lemons is an important choice that will have a big impact on the orchard's performance. Lemon trees grow best in subtropical and tropical regions; they need well-drained soil that ranges from slightly acidic to neutral pH.

Sunlight is also important; the spot should ideally receive full sun for the majority of the day. Since lemons are susceptible to severe cold, it is imperative to take into account variables like temperature, precipitation, and frost susceptibility.

Furthermore, consideration should be given to the markets' and the transportation infrastructure's proximity to optimize distribution and reduce losses after harvest.

METHODS FOR PREPARING LAND

To start a fruitful and healthy lemon orchard, the land must be prepared well. The first step is to remove any undesired vegetation, weeds, or debris from the site. Compacted soil can be broken up by plowing and subsoiling, which improves drainage and root penetration. The structure and fertility of the soil are enhanced by the addition of organic matter. Waterlogging is reduced and uniform irrigation is ensured by precision leveling. Installing appropriate drainage systems is essential to avoiding water stagnation, which can cause infections in the roots. It's important to have trees spaced appropriately apart to promote healthy airflow and sunshine exposure.

WATERING SYSTEMS FOR LEMON GROVES

For their whole growing season, lemon trees need steady, sufficient moisture. To conserve water and encourage the best possible health for trees, an effective irrigation system must be installed.

Because drip irrigation uses less water and delivers water directly to the root zone, it is frequently used in lemon orchards. It is possible to use soil moisture sensors to monitor and control irrigation schedules, avoiding over- or under-watering. Mulching the area surrounding the trees' bases aids in controlling soil temperature, weed suppression, and moisture retention. Sustainable water management techniques include choosing the right irrigation methods and giving careful consideration to the availability of water in the area.

STRATEGIES FOR MANAGING DISEASES AND PESTS

A healthy crop depends on keeping lemon orchards free from pests and illnesses. The emphasis of integrated pest management (IPM) strategies is on combining chemical, cultural, and biological control techniques. To organically manage pest populations, beneficial insects can be introduced, such as parasitoids and predatory mites. Early intervention is made possible by regularly checking orchards for symptoms of pests and illnesses. To reduce the potential harm to the environment and prevent the emergence of pesticide resistance, chemical control techniques, such as the prudent application of pesticides, must be handled carefully. Lemon cultivators may also want to think about disease-resistant types. Sanitation techniques, such as correct pruning and removing unhealthy plant material, may assist reduce the spread of diseases.

Careful site selection, thorough land preparation, effective irrigation systems, and effective pest and disease control are all necessary for a lemon grove to succeed. Lemon growers may optimize their crop yields and foster a healthy tree habitat by tackling these factors in their entirety.

CHAPTER FIVE

GROWING AND MAINTAINING LEMON TREES

TECHNIQUES FOR LEMON TREE PROPAGATION

There are several ways to multiply lemon trees, but the most popular ones are grafting, cuttings, and seeds. Although cultivating lemon trees from seeds is simple, the end product frequently differs from the parent plant. Many gardeners prefer to use cuttings or grafting for a more consistent result.

Genetically identical plants can be grown by taking cuttings from well-established, robust lemon trees and planting them in a well-prepared soil mixture. In contrast, grafting entails affixing a scion—a cutting from a lemon tree—to a rootstock.

This technique increases disease resistance and adaptation while maintaining the desired traits of the parent plant.

PLANTING TECHNIQUES AND ALIGNMENT

The general health and productivity of lemon trees depend on the location in which they are planted. Lemon trees grow best in well-drained, neutral to slightly acidic soil that receives plenty of sunlight. Digging a hole that is the same depth and twice as wide as the root ball is crucial. Add organic matter to the soil before planting to improve its drainage and fertility. For the lemon tree to have enough sunlight and airflow, proper spacing is essential. Depending on the kind, lemon trees should normally be spaced 12 to 25 feet apart. This encourages robust growth and makes maintenance chores like trimming and harvesting easier to accomplish.

CONTROLLING NUTRIENTS AND FERTILIZATION

For the best growth, lemon trees need soil that is both balanced and rich in nutrients. Frequent soil testing aids in identifying the soil's unique nutritional requirements.

It is recommended to fertilize in the spring and fall, utilizing a fertilizer that is well-balanced and has a greater nitrogen ratio. To encourage rapid vegetative development, nitrogen is essential. Furthermore, iron and zinc are two micronutrients that are necessary to counteract deficits that can cause leaf yellowing. To enhance the soil's structure and nutrient content, organic fertilizers like compost and well-rotted manure can be added. It is crucial to irrigate the soil sufficiently to keep it continuously damp but not soggy.

LEMON TREE PRUNING AND TRAINING FOR OPTIMAL GROWTH

Pruning is essential for controlling the size, fostering air circulation, and shaping lemon trees. Formative pruning helps newly planted lemon trees build a sturdy branch structure. This entails keeping a central leader and eliminating any branches that compete or cross over. Regular pruning as the tree ages aids in the removal of unhealthy or dead wood, enhancing sunlight penetration and lowering the likelihood of pests and diseases. Depending on the intended structure and available area, lemon trees can be pruned into a variety of shapes, such as central leader or open center. By encouraging the branches to grow outward instead of inward, you may optimize the amount of sunshine they receive, which promotes better fruit growth. To stop plant diseases from spreading, it's imperative to use sharp, clean pruning shears. Long-term productivity and well-being of lemon trees are enhanced by routine trimming practice monitoring and amendment.

CHAPTER SIX

HARVESTING AND HANDLING AFTER HARVEST

WHEN IS THE BEST TIME TO GATHER LEMONS?

A critical component of citrus farming is figuring out when to harvest lemons. The best time to harvest fruit depends on several variables, including fruit size, color, and flavor. When lemons have fully grown and exhibit the correct hue—which is typically a vivid yellow— they are picked. The fruit's flavor profile, which strikes a balance between sweetness and acidity, is another important sign. Fruit that is harvested too soon may not be fully grown, whereas fruit that is harvested too late may be overripe and of lower quality.

HARVESTING METHODS AND EQUIPMENT

Tools and methods for harvesting are essential to guaranteeing the effectiveness and caliber of the procedure. Lemons are often harvested by hand, with trained laborers meticulously selecting each fruit to prevent harm. For regions that are difficult to access, pole pickers can be used to ensure a complete harvest. For large-scale operations, mechanized harvesting with specialized equipment like shakers can be employed. Harvesting fruit carefully is necessary to avoid bruising or other damage that could lower its market value.

AFTER-HARVEST MANAGEMENT AND PRESERVATION

Handling and storing lemons after harvest are essential to maintaining their freshness and quality. Lemons should be transferred to packaging facilities in well-ventilated containers as soon as they are harvested to reduce temperature changes.

Processes of sorting and grading are used to eliminate fruits that are faulty or damaged. Sufficient packing, like permeable crates or boxes, aids in preserving ideal humidity levels and averts condensation, which may cause deterioration.

GRADING AND QUALITY ASSURANCE

Grading and quality control are essential steps in the post-harvest procedure. Inspections are conducted in-depth to find any flaws, illnesses, or problems that could compromise the overall quality of the fruit. Lemons are graded according to their size, color, and appearance, which enables uniform pricing and packaging. By doing this, the citrus industry's reputation is preserved and consumers' expectations are met with only the highest-quality fruits.

A combination of precise timing, practical methods, and suitable tools are needed for successful lemon harvesting. To get fresh, premium lemons to market, post-harvest handling—which includes grading, storage, and quality control—is crucial. By keeping the value of their produce intact, these methods help growers as well as the citrus industry as a whole and customer pleasure.

CHAPTER SEVEN

TECHNIQUES FOR MARKETING LEMON PRODUCTS

FINDING THE RIGHT LEMON PRODUCT TARGET MARKETS

The target markets that will be most receptive to the goods must be identified and understood to market lemon items successfully. The consumer demographic is a crucial factor to take into account since it involves identifying age groups, lifestyles, and tastes that complement products on a lemon basis. For example, a significant portion of the target market may consist of health-conscious people looking for natural, vitamin-rich substitutes. Finding marketplaces where lemons are frequently utilized in cooking, like the food and beverage sector, might also be helpful. Targeted marketing initiatives can also benefit from an understanding of the regional inclinations and cultural settings around the popularity of lemons.

Businesses can customize their strategy to efficiently reach and engage with their target audience by performing comprehensive market research.

CREATING A SIGNATURE LOOK FOR YOUR LEMON FARM

Establishing a distinct and identifiable presence in the market requires a lemon farm to have a strong brand identity. This entails creating a distinctive visual identity, including logos and package designs that capture the brightness and freshness connected to lemons, in addition to selecting an engaging and memorable brand name. Using the farm's history and core principles—such as its dedication to organic farming or sustainability—can help create a brand image that appeals to customers who care about the environment. Brand recognition and customer trust are strengthened by maintaining consistency across all brand elements, including product labeling and online presence. Furthermore, highlighting the farm's dedication to excellence and the distinctive qualities of its lemon products can set it apart from rivals and promote brand loyalty.

FORMULATING SUCCESSFUL MARKETING INITIATIVES

Creating memorable marketing campaigns is essential to raising sales and spreading the word about lemon products. Using a combination of digital and conventional marketing platforms can help campaigns reach a wider audience. Consumer attention can be piqued with interesting information that emphasizes the uses, health advantages, and recipes of lemon products. Social media platforms can be effective instruments for displaying eye-catching material and establishing direct communication with the intended audience. Working together with influencers or professionals in the food, wellness, and health domains can expand the audience and boost the legitimacy of marketing campaigns. Customers might be encouraged to test products by offering discounts, promotions, or time-limited deals, which can boost sales and brand awareness.

CHANNELS OF DISTRIBUTION AND SALES TECHNIQUES

Making the appropriate distribution channel choices is essential to guaranteeing that lemon products effectively reach their target market. Creating alliances with local markets, supermarkets, and food stores enables wide retail availability. Additionally, firms can attract customers who prefer the convenience of online buying and tap into a larger market by investigating online platforms and e-commerce channels. Building ties with wholesalers and distributors can help with effective supply chain management and guarantee a steady and dependable supply of goods to retailers. To increase exposure and promote purchases, sales strategies can incorporate product placement techniques including eye-catching displays and in-store incentives.

CHAPTER EIGHT

PROBLEMS AND REMEDIES IN LEMON PLANTING

TYPICAL OBSTACLES LEMON GROWERS FACE

Like any agricultural pursuit, growing lemons presents several difficulties that can have a big impact on the yield and financial success of lemon orchards. The vulnerability of lemon trees to pests and diseases is one common problem. Aphids, mites, and citrus leaf miners are some of the pests that frequently target citrus crops, especially lemons. This can result in decreased fruit quality and productivity. Lemon orchards are further threatened by disease outbreaks like citrus canker or greening, which call for careful management techniques.

An additional major obstacle encountered by lemon growers is the susceptibility of citrus fruits to unfavorable meteorological circumstances. Elevated temperatures, frost, and erratic precipitation patterns can have detrimental effects on lemon trees, influencing fruit development, blossoming, and the general well-being of the tree. Farmers of lemons face a constant struggle as unpredictable weather occurrences can upset the growth cycle and result in decreased yields. To reduce these risks, farmers must modify their production procedures.

For lemon growers, price instability and market swings present additional difficulties. Trade policies, supply chain interruptions, and worldwide demand are some of the variables that might impact the citrus industry. The profitability of lemon farming can be affected by price fluctuations in the market, thus farmers must implement techniques that strengthen market resilience and provide a steady income.

ECO-FRIENDLY AGRICULTURE METHODS

Sustainable agricultural practices have become essential to citrus cultivation in response to the difficulties lemon growers confront.

Using integrated pest management (IPM) techniques is a major priority to handle disease and insect problems without using chemical pesticides excessively. This strategy makes use of crop rotation, natural predators, and biological control techniques to keep the orchard's environment in balance.

Sustainable agricultural strategies for lemon growing also include maximizing soil health and water utilization. Water conservation is aided by effective irrigation technologies, including drip irrigation, which guarantees that lemon plants get the necessary moisture without wasting any. Techniques for conserving soil, including mulching and cover crops, help to keep the soil fertile, stop erosion, and improve the overall sustainability of orchards.

Lemon growers looking for greener options are increasingly adopting organic agricultural methods. The environmental effect of lemon growing can be decreased by using organic fertilizers, avoiding synthetic pesticides, and encouraging biodiversity in the orchard. These practices all lead to healthier ecosystems.

PLANNING FOR CONTINGENCIES AND RISK MANAGEMENT

The success of lemon farming operations depends on efficient risk management and backup plans, given the inherent uncertainties in agriculture. To lessen their reliance on a single product, farmers must cultivate a variety of citrus crops to diversify their risk exposure. Risks associated with the weather, disease outbreaks, and market volatility can all be mitigated by diversification.

Risk management requires the use of cutting-edge technologies and data-driven decision-making procedures. For example, weather monitoring systems offer real-time data that enables farmers to foresee and quickly adapt to unfavorable weather circumstances. In a similar vein, farmers can maximize resource consumption, boost productivity, and reduce risks related to resource mismanagement by implementing precision agriculture techniques.

For farmers growing lemons, risk management also heavily depends on financial planning and insurance programs. Programs for crop insurance can act as a safety net if unanticipated events result in yield losses, assisting farmers in recovering and maintaining their way of life. To stop the spread of disease and pest outbreaks and lessen their effects on the orchard, early detection, quick action, and quarantine procedures must be put in place.

Tackling the difficulties lemon growers confront calls for an all-encompassing strategy that includes effective risk management techniques and sustainable agricultural methods. Lemon growers can protect their livelihoods in the face of uncertainty, strengthen the resilience of their orchards, and advance environmental sustainability by adopting these ideas.

CHAPTER NINE

RULES AND ADHERENCE

COMPREHENDING AGRICULTURAL REGULATIONS

Agricultural regulations comprise a multifaceted structure of guidelines and standards intended to control several facets of farming operations. These rules are meant to preserve consumer health and welfare, preserve the environment, and guarantee the sustainability of agricultural practices. Agriculture is governed by a wide range of laws at the municipal, state, and federal levels of government. Numerous topics are covered by these regulations, such as food safety, pesticide use, land use, and water management.

It is a complex network of rules that farmers must understand to follow the law and manage their farms responsibly. A violation of agricultural regulations may result in fines, legal repercussions, or even the cessation of farming operations. Farmers must comprehend these standards, as doing so not only keeps them out of legal hot water but also enhances the agricultural industry's general resilience and longevity.

ENVIRONMENTAL COMPLIANCE IN LEMON FARMING

Environmental laws designed to lessen the effects of farming operations on the environment apply to lemon farming, just like they do to other agricultural pursuits. In lemon farming, environmental compliance includes following the regulations on water use, conserving soil, and using agrochemicals sensibly. For example, saving water is essential since lemons frequently need a lot of water to grow to their full potential. Adherence to water consumption restrictions guarantees sustainable farming methods that do not exhaust nearby water supplies.

Additionally, using fertilizers and pesticides responsibly is crucial to adhering to environmental regulations. To reduce their detrimental effects on the quality of the soil and water, regulations frequently specify the kinds and quantities of agrochemicals that can be used. To preserve a balance between agricultural output and environmental protection, integrated pest management (IPM) practices—which emphasize natural pest control measures in addition to the prudent use of chemicals—are frequently promoted.

BEST PRACTICES AND SAFETY STANDARDS

In agriculture, safety regulations are essential for safeguarding agricultural laborers and consumers alike. Lemon farming requires several potentially dangerous tasks, including using machinery, working with chemicals, and being outside in the elements. Adherence to safety protocols is crucial to avert mishaps, harm, and chronic health complications linked to agricultural labor.

Using personal protection equipment (PPE), implementing safe work procedures, and providing farm workers with the necessary training are all necessary to ensure that safety regulations are followed. Establishing a secure working environment also involves routine maintenance and inspection of farm equipment. The creation of emergency response plans and the availability of first aid supplies are also essential elements in guaranteeing the safety of individuals engaged in lemon-growing activities.

The goal of best safety practices is ongoing improvement rather than merely following the law. To stay up to date on the newest safety precautions and technologies, farmers frequently participate in continuing education and training. Working together in the agricultural community and forming alliances with regulatory agencies can help cultivate a safety culture that puts everyone's health and safety—from the fields to the consumers—as a top priority in addition to complying with the law.

CHAPTER TEN

TRENDS IN LEMON FARMING GOING FORWARD

New Developments in Agricultural Technologies: The use of new technology in agriculture will have a big impact on lemon cultivation in the future. Lemon farming is becoming more and more reliant on precision farming, which makes use of cutting-edge sensors, GPS, and data analytics.

Multispectral imaging-equipped drones can deliver real-time data on crop health, enabling farmers to see possible problems like infections or nutrient deficits early on. Furthermore, robotics and automated equipment are increasingly essential to lemon farming, simplifying operations like pruning and harvesting. These technologies not only improve productivity but also help minimize environmental impact and optimize resource use.

TRENDS IN ORGANIC AND SUSTAINABLE AGRICULTURE

One major factor influencing lemon farming's future is sustainability. Farmers are implementing sustainable techniques that reduce the use of synthetic inputs and give priority to ecological balance as environmental conservation gains more and more attention. Particularly organic lemon farming is becoming more and more popular as people become more aware of where their food comes from.

Agroforestry, cover crops, and integrated pest management are a few of the sustainable techniques that are becoming popular. In addition, water-saving methods like rainwater collection and drip irrigation are essential for encouraging sustainable lemon growing.

Incorporating these approaches not only guarantees a more robust ecosystem but also satisfies the market's increasing need for lemons that are produced sustainably.

NOVELTIES IN LEMON VARIETALS AND AGRICULTURAL METHODS

Developments in citrus cultivation methods and lemon cultivars will influence citrus agriculture in the future. Researchers and breeders are working to create lemon types with superior flavor profiles, increased productivity, and increased resistance to illnesses. It is being investigated to use genetic engineering to produce variants with desired characteristics that provide resistance to pests and environmental stressors. Furthermore, new lemon cultivar development is accelerated through the use of precision breeding techniques. To maximize space efficiency and boost overall productivity, farmers are also implementing cutting-edge agricultural techniques including vertical farming and high-density planting. These developments enable growers to adjust to shifting market needs and environmental conditions in addition to broadening the range of lemon types that are currently accessible.

New developments in lemon types and farming methods, the integration of developing technologies, and sustainable practices are all critical to the future of lemon farming. Lemon growers are well-positioned to take advantage of these developments in the agricultural landscape to secure the sustainability and prosperity of their citrus farming ventures in the long run.

www.ingramcontent.com/pod-product-compliance
Lightning Source LLC
Chambersburg PA
CBHW070824290526
45795CB00002B/834